★ THE ★
UNITED
STATES
PRESIDENTS

ZACHARY TAYLOR

Heidi M.D. Elston

Checkerboard
Library

An Imprint of Abdo Publishing
abdobooks.com

ABDOBOOKS.COM

Published by Abdo Publishing, a division of ABDO, PO Box 398166, Minneapolis, Minnesota 55439. Copyright © 2021 by Abdo Consulting Group, Inc. International copyrights reserved in all countries. No part of this book may be reproduced in any form without written permission from the publisher. Checkerboard Library™ is a trademark and logo of Abdo Publishing.

Printed in the United States of America, North Mankato, Minnesota
052020
092020

THIS BOOK CONTAINS RECYCLED MATERIALS

Design: Emily O'Malley, Kelly Doudna, Mighty Media, Inc.
Production: Mighty Media, Inc.
Editor: Jessica Rusick

Cover Photograph: Stock Montage/Getty Images
Interior Photographs: Albert de Bruijn/iStockphoto, p. 37; AP Images, p. 36; Getty Images, p. 23; Hulton Archive/Getty Images, pp. 11, 29; Library of Congress, pp. 7, 13, 15, 16, 21, 22, 24, 27, 30, 31, 33, 40; North Wind Picture Archives, pp. 6 (Chief Black Hawk), 7 (capture of Monterrey), 14, 17, 18, 19, 20; Pete Souza/Flickr, p. 44; Shutterstock Images, pp. 5, 7 (Taylor oval portrait), 25, 38, 39; Wikimedia Commons, pp. 6, 12, 32, 40 (Washington), 42

Library of Congress Control Number: 2019956552

Publisher's Cataloging-in-Publication Data
Names: Elston, Heidi M.D., author.
Title: Zachary Taylor / by Heidi M.D. Elston
Description: Minneapolis, Minnesota : Abdo Publishing, 2021 | Series: The United States presidents | Includes online resources and index.
Identifiers: ISBN 9781532193743 (lib. bdg.) | ISBN 9781098212384 (ebook)
Subjects: LCSH: Taylor, Zachary, 1784-1850--Juvenile literature. | Presidents--Biography--Juvenile literature. | Presidents--United States--History--Juvenile literature. | Legislators--United States—Biography--Juvenile literature. | Politics and government--Biography--Juvenile literature.
Classification: DDC 973.63092--dc23

★ CONTENTS ★

Zachary Taylor.........................4

Timeline 6

Did You Know?........................9

Young Zachary........................10

Military Family 12

A Great War Hero 14

War with Mexico 16

The Election of 1848.................20

The Twelfth President................24

President Taylor's Cabinet...........26

The Slavery Debate Continues 28

A Sudden Death......................32

Office of the President...............34

Presidents and Their Terms.........40

Glossary 46

Online Resources....................47

Index 48

Zachary Taylor

Zachary Taylor was the twelfth president of the United States. Before becoming president, Taylor had no political experience. He was the first person without previous political experience to become president.

Though he did not have political experience, Taylor had served his country for 40 years as a soldier. He had proved himself a good and able leader.

Taylor was elected president in 1848. At that time, the United States was growing. Americans were arguing over slavery. Taylor owned more than 100 slaves. But he did not believe that new states should allow slavery.

Because of his views, Southerners were unhappy with Taylor. They wanted new states to allow slavery. The South began talking about leaving the United States.

President Taylor strongly opposed this. He wanted to maintain unity. But Taylor never saw the end of the struggle over slavery. He died just 16 months after his **inauguration**.

TIMELINE

1810

Taylor married Margaret Mackall Smith. Taylor was promoted to captain in the army.

1784

On November 24, Zachary Taylor was born in Orange County, Virginia.

1837

Taylor defeated the Seminole Native Americans at Lake Okeechobee, Florida.

1808

Taylor joined the US Army as a first lieutenant.

1819

Taylor became a lieutenant colonel.

1832

Taylor fought in the Black Hawk War and won the surrender of Chief Black Hawk.

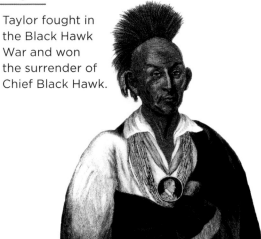

1850

The Clayton-Bulwer Treaty was signed on April 19. On July 9, Zachary Taylor died.

1846

Taylor began fighting in the Mexican-American War.

1848

The Whig Party nominated Taylor to run for president.

1841

Taylor became the commander at Fort Smith in Arkansas.

1847

Taylor became an American hero after the battle at Buena Vista. He returned to his Louisiana plantation.

1849

On March 5, Taylor became the twelfth US president.

"I am conscious that the position which I have been called to fill, though sufficient to satisfy the loftiest ambition, is **surrounded by fearful responsibilities.**"

ZACHARY TAYLOR

DID YOU KNOW?

★ James Madison was Zachary Taylor's second cousin. Madison served as the fourth president of the United States from 1809 to 1817.

★ Taylor moved around often as a military man. Because of that, he never voted in any election!

★ Abraham Lincoln served under Colonel Taylor in the Black Hawk War.

★ President Taylor took his horse, Old Whitey, with him to the White House. Old Whitey grazed on the White House lawn.

★ The 1848 presidential election made US history. For the first time, all states voted at the same time.

Young Zachary

Zachary Taylor was born in Orange County, Virginia, on November 24, 1784. He was the third of nine children. Zachary had five brothers and three sisters.

Zachary's parents were Richard Taylor and Sarah Strother Taylor. Both Richard and Sarah came from wealthy families. Richard had been an army officer in the **American Revolution**. Sarah was well educated. She had received her schooling from **tutors**.

In 1785, the Taylor family moved into what is now northern Kentucky. There, Zachary grew up on a plantation in Jefferson County.

The Taylor family was loving. Zachary's brothers and sisters were his close friends. At that time, there were no schools on the frontier. So, the Taylor children studied with a tutor at home. They also received schooling from their parents.

★

FAST FACTS

BORN: November 24, 1784

WIFE: Margaret Mackall Smith (1788–1852)

CHILDREN: 6

POLITICAL PARTY: Whig

AGE AT INAUGURATION: 64

YEARS SERVED: 1849–1850

VICE PRESIDENT: Millard Fillmore

DIED: July 9, 1850, age 65

Zachary's birthplace in Virginia

Richard told his children stories about his service in the war. Zachary decided he wanted to be in the military too. So did most of his brothers. In fact, all but one joined the army. Zachary would later become a famous military hero.

Military Family

In 1808, Taylor joined the US Army as a first lieutenant. He became a captain in 1810. That same year, Taylor met and married Margaret Mackall Smith. Margaret had been born in Calvert County, Maryland, in 1788.

The Taylors had five daughters and a son. Two daughters, Octavia and Margaret, died young. The three remaining daughters, Sarah, Ann, and Mary Elizabeth, married military men. The Taylors' son, Richard, was a lieutenant general in the **Confederate** army.

— Margaret Taylor —

Sarah married Jefferson Davis. Sadly, she died just three months after the wedding. Davis later served as president of the Confederate States of America.

Ann married a US Army surgeon named Robert Wood. Wood had served with Taylor in the military. Mary Elizabeth married Colonel William Wallace Bliss. Bliss was Taylor's military aide. He later served as Taylor's secretary during his presidency.

Richard Taylor

A Great War Hero

During the **War of 1812**, Taylor served at frontier posts in **Indiana Territory.** There, he defended Fort Harrison.

Chief Black Hawk's Native American name is Ma-ka-tai-me-she-kia-kiak.

Taylor was rewarded for his bravery with a promotion to major. In 1819, he became a lieutenant colonel.

Taylor later served in Wisconsin during the **Black Hawk War** of 1832. American soldiers defeated Native Americans in this conflict. Taylor won the surrender of Chief Black Hawk. And, the United States received Native American lands in Illinois.

Taylor was a popular and respected military leader. Although he was a high-ranking officer, he wore a plain uniform. And, he often placed himself close to enemy fire. Taylor's men gave him the nickname "Old Rough and Ready."

In 1837, Taylor defeated the Seminole Native Americans at Lake Okeechobee, Florida. Because of this victory, Taylor was made a brigadier general. In 1841, Taylor became commander at Fort Smith in Arkansas. He later commanded Fort Jesup in Louisiana.

Old Rough and Ready and his horse, Old Whitey

War with Mexico

Meanwhile, tensions between the United States and Mexico were mounting. In 1845, the United States **annexed** Texas and made it a state. This angered Mexico.

Then, the two countries disagreed about Texas's southwestern border. The United States said a river called the Rio Grande served as the boundary. But Mexico claimed the boundary was the Nueces River. Both nations prepared for war.

President James K. Polk

In 1846, President James K. Polk sent General Taylor to Texas. Taylor and his men were stationed on the land between the Rio Grande and the Nueces River.

The **Mexican-American War** began on May 13. Taylor and his soldiers then entered Mexico. They occupied Matamoros on May 18. On September 24, they captured the city of Monterrey.

Capture of Monterrey

In 1847, President Polk decided to move an army to Veracruz. From there, the United States would attack Mexico City. Polk ordered many of Taylor's men to move to this new position. They were now under the command of Major General Winfield Scott.

The Mexican army learned of the US plans. It decided to attack Taylor at Buena Vista. Taylor's army was outnumbered. But they still won the battle! The victory made Taylor an American hero.

Mexican and American leaders signed a peace treaty on February 2, 1848. Mexico had to sell the United States thousands of square miles of land. The United States paid $15 million for it.

This land became known as the Mexican Cession. It included today's California, Nevada, and Utah. Parts of Arizona, Colorado, New Mexico, and Wyoming were also included in this deal.

A map showing the land the United States acquired after the war

MAP SHOWING THE TERRITORY ACQUIRED FROM MEXICO AS THE RESULT OF THE MEXICAN WAR

At Buena Vista, Taylor's army numbered about 5,000 men. Still, they defeated between 16,000 and 20,000 Mexican troops.

6

The Election of 1848

In 1847, Taylor had returned to his Louisiana plantation. The 1848 US presidential election approached. Many Americans thought Taylor should run for president.

Lewis Cass

However, he was not interested in seeking election. Taylor was content to stay home and farm. But he agreed to run if the nomination was offered to him.

The **Whigs** held their national **convention** in Philadelphia, Pennsylvania, in 1848. They nominated Taylor to run for president. Millard Fillmore of New York was chosen as his **running mate**. The **Democrats** chose Senator Lewis Cass of Michigan to oppose Taylor. His **running mate** was General William Butler of Kentucky.

During the campaign, the expansion of slavery was an important issue. Cass felt that new territories should decide for themselves if they wanted slavery.

Because of Cass's views on slavery, his nomination angered many Northern **Democrats**. They were working to end slavery in America. Many of the unhappy Democrats

William Butler

started a new political party. They called it the **Free-Soil** Party. They chose former president Martin Van Buren to run for president.

Taylor campaigned hard. He reminded voters of his military record. This attracted many Northern voters. Although slavery was a key issue, Taylor rarely expressed his views on this topic. However, he owned more than 100 slaves. This appealed to many Southern voters.

In November 1848, Americans voted. Taylor and Fillmore won the election. They received 163 electoral votes, while Cass and Butler won 127. Van Buren received none.

Taylor and Fillmore had won eight slave states and seven free states. Cass and his **running mate** had won seven slave states and eight free states.

Martin Van Buren was president from 1837 to 1841.

FOR PRESIDENT OF THE PEOPLE

ZACHARY TAYLOR

About party creeds let party zealots fight
He cant be wrong whose life is in the right .—

A Taylor campaign banner

7

The Twelfth President

On March 5, 1849, Taylor was **inaugurated** as the twelfth **president of the United States.** Normally, he would have taken office on March 4. However, Taylor did not want to be inaugurated on a Sunday.

Taylor's greatest accomplishment as president was in foreign affairs. Under President Polk, the United States had gained land on the Pacific Coast. Now, the United States wanted to build a canal across Nicaragua. The waterway would connect the Atlantic and Pacific oceans. Great Britain was also interested in building a canal.

Secretary of State John M. Clayton met with Sir Henry Bulwer of Great Britain. The two men arranged an important treaty. Both countries agreed to keep the canal **neutral** once it was built. The Clayton-Bulwer Treaty was signed on April 19, 1850.

John M. Clayton

Taylor was the first president elected after
the Mexican-American War.

PRESIDENT TAYLOR'S CABINET

ONE TERM

March 5, 1849–July 9, 1850

- ★ **STATE:** John M. Clayton
- ★ **TREASURY:** William Morris Meredith
- ★ **WAR:** George Washington Crawford
- ★ **NAVY:** William Ballard Preston
- ★ **ATTORNEY GENERAL:** Reverdy Johnson
- ★ **INTERIOR:** Thomas Ewing (from March 8, 1849)

President Zachary Taylor (*center*) and his cabinet

8

The Slavery Debate Continues

Once he took office, President Taylor voiced his views on slavery. He believed that people in the South should be allowed to keep their slaves.

But Taylor also believed that new states and territories should not allow slavery. Many southerners felt betrayed by President Taylor's beliefs. Taylor's views did not solve the slavery issue. In fact, more problems developed.

In 1849, California wanted to join the United States as a free state. President Taylor asked Congress to approve this request. However, some Southern congressmen wanted slavery to be allowed in California. This started much **debate** in Congress.

Southerners were not happy. Some Southern leaders wanted the South to become a new and separate country. But President Taylor did not want this to happen. He promised to use force to keep the United States of America together.

Henry Clay

Millard Fillmore served as president from 1850 to 1853.

Many congressmen considered ways to compromise on the slavery issue. On January 29, 1850, Senator Henry Clay of Kentucky presented his ideas to Congress. Clay thought it would be good if some new states allowed slavery.

President Taylor did not support Clay's compromise. He stood firm against new slave states. The slavery **debate** continued. Northern and Southern senators argued with each other. It seemed to many that the slavery problem would never be solved.

The congressmen who supported compromise would eventually win. However, they would not see victory until Vice President Fillmore became president.

Taylor delivered his annual message to Congress on December 4, 1849. In it, he said it would be the "greatest of calamities" if the United States broke apart.

9

A Sudden Death

On July 4, 1850, President Taylor attended a Fourth of July celebration in Washington, DC. That evening, he became sick. Taylor stayed in bed for five days, but he did not improve. On July 9, President Zachary Taylor died. He was buried near Louisville, Kentucky.

Taylor was in office for only 16 months. Vice President Fillmore became president following Taylor's death. The slavery **debate** continued. Two months later, Senator Clay's ideas about slavery became law. These laws are called the Compromise of 1850.

Taylor served his country for more than 40 years. He was a well-respected, successful, and brave military leader. Taylor proved to be a courageous president as well. He took a firm stand against the spread of slavery in America. Zachary Taylor fought to maintain the United States of America that he loved.

— Taylor is buried in the Zachary — Taylor National Cemetery.

Taylor was the second president to die in office.

BRANCHES OF GOVERNMENT

The US government is divided into three branches. They are the executive, legislative, and judicial branches. This division is called a separation of powers. Each branch has some power over the others. This is called a system of checks and balances.

★ EXECUTIVE BRANCH

The executive branch enforces laws. It is made up of the president, the vice president, and the president's cabinet. The president represents the United States around the world. He or she oversees relations with other countries and signs treaties. The president signs bills into law and appoints officials and federal judges. He or she also leads the military and manages government workers.

★ LEGISLATIVE BRANCH

The legislative branch makes laws, maintains the military, and regulates trade. It also has the power to declare war. This branch consists of the Senate and the House of Representatives. Together, these two houses make up Congress. Each state has two senators. A state's population determines the number of representatives it has.

★ JUDICIAL BRANCH

The judicial branch interprets laws. It consists of district courts, courts of appeals, and the Supreme Court. District courts try cases. If a person disagrees with a trial's outcome, he or she may appeal. If a court of appeals supports the ruling, a person may appeal to the Supreme Court. The Supreme Court also makes sure that laws follow the US Constitution.

THE PRESIDENT ★

★ QUALIFICATIONS FOR OFFICE

To be president, a person must meet three requirements. A candidate must be at least 35 years old and a natural-born US citizen. He or she must also have lived in the United States for at least 14 years.

★ ELECTORAL COLLEGE

The US presidential election is an indirect election. Voters from each state choose electors to represent them in the Electoral College. The number of electors from each state is based on the state's population. Each elector has one electoral vote. Electors are pledged to cast their vote for the candidate who receives the highest number of popular votes in their state. A candidate must receive the majority of Electoral College votes to win.

★ TERM OF OFFICE

Each president may be elected to two four-year terms. Sometimes, a president may only be elected once. This happens if he or she served more than two years of the previous president's term.

The presidential election is held on the Tuesday after the first Monday in November. The president is sworn in on January 20 of the following year. At that time, he or she takes the oath of office:

> *I do solemnly swear (or affirm) that I will faithfully execute the office of President of the United States, and will to the best of my ability, preserve, protect and defend the Constitution of the United States.*

LINE OF SUCCESSION

The Presidential Succession Act of 1947 defines who becomes president if the president cannot serve. The vice president is first in the line of succession. Next are the Speaker of the House and the President Pro Tempore of the Senate. If none of these individuals is able to serve, the office falls to the president's cabinet members. They would take office in the order in which each department was created:

Secretary of State

Secretary of the Treasury

Secretary of Defense

Attorney General

Secretary of the Interior

Secretary of Agriculture

Secretary of Commerce

Secretary of Labor

Secretary of Health and Human Services

Secretary of Housing and Urban Development

Secretary of Transportation

Secretary of Energy

Secretary of Education

Secretary of Veterans Affairs

Secretary of Homeland Security

While in office, the president receives a salary of $400,000 each year. He or she lives in the White House and has 24-hour Secret Service protection.

The president may travel on a Boeing 747 jet called Air Force One. The airplane can accommodate 76 passengers. It has kitchens, a dining room, sleeping areas, and a conference room. It also has fully equipped offices with the latest communications systems. Air Force One can fly halfway around the world before needing to refuel. It can even refuel in flight!

Air Force One

If the president wishes to travel by car, he or she uses Cadillac One. It has been modified with heavy armor and communications systems. The president takes

Cadillac One

Cadillac One along when visiting other countries if secure transportation will be needed.

The president also travels on a helicopter called Marine One. Like the presidential car, Marine One accompanies the president when traveling abroad if necessary.

Sometimes, the president needs to get away and relax with family and friends. Camp David is the official presidential retreat. It is located in the cool, wooded mountains of Maryland. The US Navy maintains the retreat, and the US Marine Corps keeps it secure. The camp offers swimming, tennis, golf, and hiking.

When the president leaves office, he or she receives lifetime Secret Service protection. He or she also receives a yearly pension of $207,800 and funding for office space, supplies, and staff.

Marine One

	PRESIDENT	PARTY	TOOK OFFICE
1	George Washington	None	April 30, 1789
2	John Adams	Federalist	March 4, 1797
3	Thomas Jefferson	Democratic-Republican	March 4, 1801
4	James Madison	Democratic-Republican	March 4, 1809
5	James Monroe	Democratic-Republican	March 4, 1817
6	John Quincy Adams	Democratic-Republican	March 4, 1825
7	Andrew Jackson	Democrat	March 4, 1829
8	Martin Van Buren	Democrat	March 4, 1837
9	William H. Harrison	Whig	March 4, 1841
10	John Tyler	Whig	April 6, 1841
11	James K. Polk	Democrat	March 4, 1845
12	Zachary Taylor	Whig	March 5, 1849
13	Millard Fillmore	Whig	July 10, 1850
14	Franklin Pierce	Democrat	March 4, 1853
15	James Buchanan	Democrat	March 4, 1857
16	Abraham Lincoln	Republican	March 4, 1861
17	Andrew Johnson	Democrat	April 15, 1865
18	Ulysses S. Grant	Republican	March 4, 1869
19	Rutherford B. Hayes	Republican	March 3, 1877

George Washington

Abraham Lincoln

Theodore Roosevelt

THEIR TERMS

LEFT OFFICE	TERMS SERVED	VICE PRESIDENT
March 4, 1797	Two	John Adams
March 4, 1801	One	Thomas Jefferson
March 4, 1809	Two	Aaron Burr, George Clinton
March 4, 1817	Two	George Clinton, Elbridge Gerry
March 4, 1825	Two	Daniel D. Tompkins
March 4, 1829	One	John C. Calhoun
March 4, 1837	Two	John C. Calhoun, Martin Van Buren
March 4, 1841	One	Richard M. Johnson
April 4, 1841	Died During First Term	John Tyler
March 4, 1845	Completed Harrison's Term	Office Vacant
March 4, 1849	One	George M. Dallas
July 9, 1850	Died During First Term	Millard Fillmore
March 4, 1853	Completed Taylor's Term	Office Vacant
March 4, 1857	One	William R.D. King
March 4, 1861	One	John C. Breckinridge
April 15, 1865	Served One Term, Died During Second Term	Hannibal Hamlin, Andrew Johnson
March 4, 1869	Completed Lincoln's Second Term	Office Vacant
March 4, 1877	Two	Schuyler Colfax, Henry Wilson
March 4, 1881	One	William A. Wheeler

Franklin D. Roosevelt

John F. Kennedy

Ronald Reagan

	PRESIDENT	PARTY	TOOK OFFICE
20	James A. Garfield	Republican	March 4, 1881
21	Chester Arthur	Republican	September 20, 1881
22	Grover Cleveland	Democrat	March 4, 1885
23	Benjamin Harrison	Republican	March 4, 1889
24	Grover Cleveland	Democrat	March 4, 1893
25	William McKinley	Republican	March 4, 1897
26	Theodore Roosevelt	Republican	September 14, 1901
27	William Taft	Republican	March 4, 1909
28	Woodrow Wilson	Democrat	March 4, 1913
29	Warren G. Harding	Republican	March 4, 1921
30	Calvin Coolidge	Republican	August 3, 1923
31	Herbert Hoover	Republican	March 4, 1929
32	Franklin D. Roosevelt	Democrat	March 4, 1933
33	Harry S. Truman	Democrat	April 12, 1945
34	Dwight D. Eisenhower	Republican	January 20, 1953
35	John F. Kennedy	Democrat	January 20, 1961

LEFT OFFICE	TERMS SERVED	VICE PRESIDENT
September 19, 1881	Died During First Term	Chester Arthur
March 4, 1885	Completed Garfield's Term	Office Vacant
March 4, 1889	One	Thomas A. Hendricks
March 4, 1893	One	Levi P. Morton
March 4, 1897	One	Adlai E. Stevenson
September 14, 1901	Served One Term, Died During Second Term	Garret A. Hobart, Theodore Roosevelt
March 4, 1909	Completed McKinley's Second Term, Served One Term	Office Vacant, Charles Fairbanks
March 4, 1913	One	James S. Sherman
March 4, 1921	Two	Thomas R. Marshall
August 2, 1923	Died During First Term	Calvin Coolidge
March 4, 1929	Completed Harding's Term, Served One Term	Office Vacant, Charles Dawes
March 4, 1933	One	Charles Curtis
April 12, 1945	Served Three Terms, Died During Fourth Term	John Nance Garner, Henry A. Wallace, Harry S. Truman
January 20, 1953	Completed Roosevelt's Fourth Term, Served One Term	Office Vacant, Alben Barkley
January 20, 1961	Two	Richard Nixon
November 22, 1963	Died During First Term	Lyndon B. Johnson

	PRESIDENT	PARTY	TOOK OFFICE
36	Lyndon B. Johnson	Democrat	November 22, 1963
37	Richard Nixon	Republican	January 20, 1969
38	Gerald Ford	Republican	August 9, 1974
39	Jimmy Carter	Democrat	January 20, 1977
40	Ronald Reagan	Republican	January 20, 1981
41	George H.W. Bush	Republican	January 20, 1989
42	Bill Clinton	Democrat	January 20, 1993
43	George W. Bush	Republican	January 20, 2001
44	Barack Obama	Democrat	January 20, 2009
45	Donald Trump	Republican	January 20, 2017

Barack Obama

PRESIDENTS MATH GAME

Have fun with this presidents math game! First, study the list above and memorize each president's name and number. Then, use math to figure out which president completes each equation below.

1. John F. Kennedy − Zachary Taylor = ?

2. Zachary Taylor + James Buchanan = ?

3. George H.W. Bush − Zachary Taylor = ?

Answers: 1. Benjamin Harrison (35 − 12 = 23)
2. William Taft (12 + 15 = 27)
3. Warren G. Harding (41 − 12 = 29)

LEFT OFFICE	TERMS SERVED	VICE PRESIDENT
January 20, 1969	Completed Kennedy's Term, Served One Term	Office Vacant, Hubert H. Humphrey
August 9, 1974	Completed First Term, Resigned During Second Term	Spiro T. Agnew, Gerald Ford
January 20, 1977	Completed Nixon's Second Term	Nelson A. Rockefeller
January 20, 1981	One	Walter Mondale
January 20, 1989	Two	George H.W. Bush
January 20, 1993	One	Dan Quayle
January 20, 2001	Two	Al Gore
January 20, 2009	Two	Dick Cheney
January 20, 2017	Two	Joe Biden
		Mike Pence

★ WRITE TO THE PRESIDENT ★

You may write to the president at:

**The White House
1600 Pennsylvania Avenue NW
Washington, DC 20500**

You may email the president at:

www.whitehouse.gov/contact

★ GLOSSARY ★

American Revolution—from 1775 to 1783. A war for independence between Great Britain and its North American colonies. The colonists won and created the United States of America.

annex—to take land and add it to a nation.

Black Hawk War—in 1832, a conflict between Native Americans and the US government over land in Illinois.

Confederate—relating to the Confederate States of America. This country was formed by the states of South Carolina, Georgia, Florida, Alabama, Louisiana, Mississippi, Texas, Virginia, Tennessee, Arkansas, and North Carolina when they left the Union between 1860 and 1861.

convention—a meeting of a political party's delegates to formulate a platform and select candidates for office.

debate—a contest in which two sides argue for or against something.

Democrat—a member of the Democratic political party. When Zachary Taylor was president, Democrats supported farmers and landowners.

Free-Soil—a political party that had power between 1848 and 1854. Its members opposed the extension of slavery into US territories and the admission of slave states into the Union.

inaugurate (ih-NAW-gyuh-rayt)—to swear into a political office. A ceremony in which a person is sworn into office is an inauguration.

Mexican-American War—a war fought between the United States and Mexico from 1846 to 1848.

neutral—not taking sides in a conflict.

running mate—a candidate running for a lower-rank position on an election ticket, especially the candidate for vice president.

secretary of state—a member of the president's cabinet who handles relations with other countries.

tutor—someone who teaches a student privately.

War of 1812—from 1812 to 1815. A war fought between the United States and Great Britain over shipping rights and the capture of US soldiers.

Whig—a member of a political party that was very strong in the early 1800s but ended in the 1850s. Whigs supported laws that helped business.

ONLINE RESOURCES

Booklinks
NONFICTION NETWORK
FREE! ONLINE NONFICTION RESOURCES

To learn more about Zachary Taylor, please visit **abdobooklinks.com** or scan this QR code. These links are routinely monitored and updated to provide the most current information available.

★ INDEX ★

A
American Revolution, 10

B
birth, 10
Black Hawk, Chief, 14
Black Hawk War, 14, 15
Bliss, William Wallace, 12
Bulwer, Henry, 24
Butler, William, 21, 22

C
California, 18, 28
Cass, Lewis, 20, 21, 22
childhood, 10, 11
Clay, Henry, 30, 32
Clayton, John M., 24
Clayton-Bulwer Treaty, 24
Compromise of 1850, 32
Congress, US, 28, 30

D
Davis, Jefferson, 12
death, 32
Democratic Party, 20, 21

E
education, 10

F
family, 10, 11, 12
Fillmore, Millard, 20, 22, 30, 32
Free-Soil Party, 21

M
Mexican Cession, 18
Mexican-American War, 16, 18
military service, 4, 11, 12, 14, 15, 16, 18, 32

P
Polk, James K., 16, 18, 24

S
Scott, Winfield, 18
slavery, 4, 21, 22, 28, 30, 32

T
Texas, 16

V
Van Buren, Martin, 21, 22

W
War of 1812, 14
Washington, DC, 32

31901067523623